Tiny Life on Plants

By Karin Lindstrom

Consultants

Reading Adviser
Nanci Vargus, EdD
Assistant Professor of Literacy
University of Indianapolis
Indianapolis, Indiana

Subject Adviser
Howard A. Shuman, PhD
Department of Microbiology
Columbia University Medical Center
New York, New York

Children's Press®
A Division of Scholastic Inc.
New York Toronto London Auckland Sydney
Mexico City New Delhi Hong Kong
Danbury, Connecticut

Designer: Herman Adler Design
Photo Researcher: Caroline Anderson
The photo on the cover shows nitrogen-fixing bacteria in the cells of a plant.

Library of Congress Cataloging-in-Publication Data

Lindstrom, Karin, 1966–
    Tiny life on plants / by Karin Lindstrom ; consultant, Nanci R. Vargus.
        p. cm. — (Rookie read-about science)
    Includes index.
    ISBN 0-516-25297-6 (lib. bdg.)   0-516-25478-2 (pbk.)
    1. Plants—Microbiology—Juvenile literature. I. Vargus, Nanci Reginelli. II.
Title. III. Series.
    QR351.L54 2005
    577.8'52—dc22   2005004632

CHILDREN'S PRESS, and ROOKIE READ-ABOUT®,
and associated logos are trademarks and/or registered trademarks
of Scholastic Library Publishing. SCHOLASTIC and associated logos
are trademarks and/or registered trademarks of Scholastic Inc.

1 2 3 4 5 6 7 8 9 10 R 14 13 12 11 10 09 08 07 06 05

Trees are the largest living things on Earth.

Trees can change. Tiny bacteria (bak-TIHR-ee-uh) can change big trees.

Bacteria are very small. You need a microscope to see them.

A spoonful of soil may have more than 1 billion bacteria.

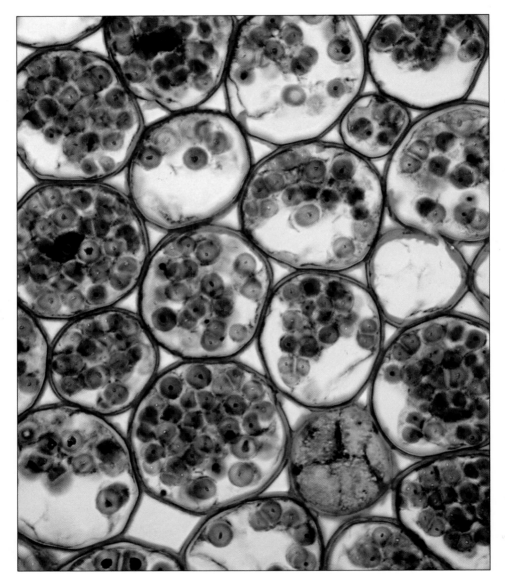

6

Bacteria must eat to live.
Some bacteria make food
from sunlight. Others
eat things that are living
or dead.

Some bacteria eat bugs.

Fire ants are bugs that eat crops. They hurt the crops by eating them.

A bacteria eats the ants without hurting the crops!

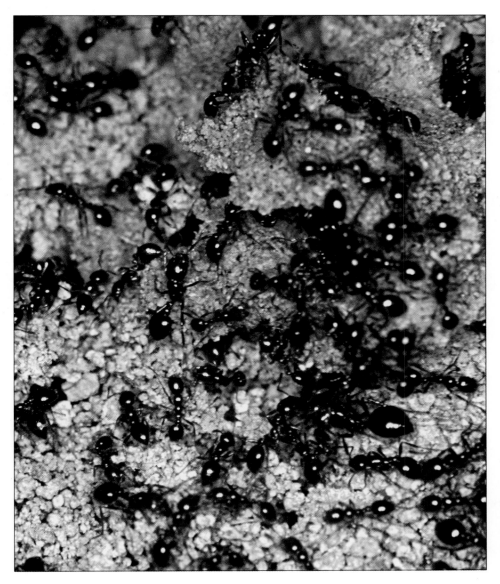

10

Some bacteria live in the roots of beans and pea plants. They also live on the roots of trees.

These bacteria help plants and trees grow strong.

Another kind of tiny life
is fungus.

Funguses must eat dead
or living things. Funguses
can't make food from
sunlight like plants can.

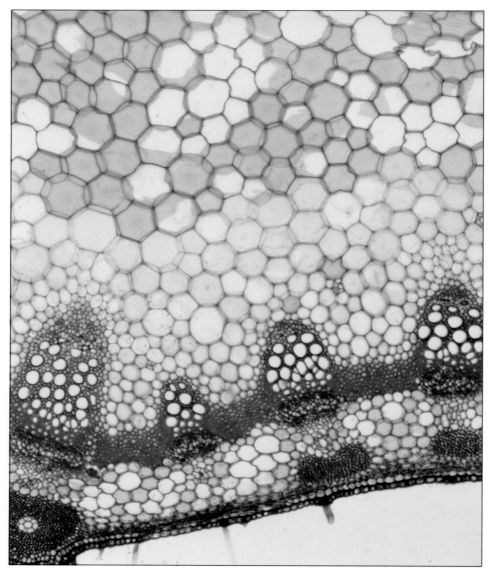

14

Plants and trees are made up of thousands of parts called cells (SELLS).

Bacteria are made up of only one cell. Some funguses also have only one cell.

A fungus can also have many cells. The cells group together, and the fungus grows.

This fungus can grow as big as a soccer ball!

18

A mushroom is a type
of fungus.

It lives under the ground.
Sometimes it pushes up
out of the ground.

Mushrooms come in many
shapes, sizes, and colors.

One fungus lives on the roots of some plants. It helps bring food and water to the roots.

This fungus helps bananas, mangoes, and sweet potatoes.

21

22

Funguses also help flowers.

Many orchid flowers will not grow unless they have a fungus on their roots.

Some kinds of fungus
help people. People use the
fungus to make medicine.

This fungus is used to make
a medicine called penicillin.

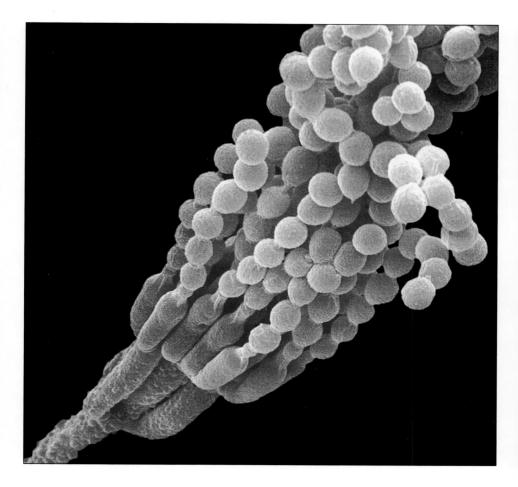

26

Not all funguses are helpful.

More than 100 years ago,
a fungus killed Ireland's
potatoes. People had no
potatoes to eat. Millions
of people died.

Bacteria and fungus are tiny kinds of life.

Even though they are small, they play a big role on Earth.

29

Words You Know

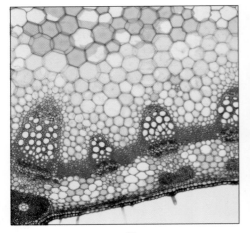

cells

mushroom

orchid

soil   tree

Index

About the Author

Karin Lindstrom is a writer from Lenexa, Kansas, where she lives with her husband and son. When she's not gardening among the microbes, she enjoys reading to students and helping them find books in the library. Karin graduated with a bachelors of science degree in physical therapy and worked for ten years as a physical therapist, before launching a career in writing. She has always been fascinated with the many facets of science, beginning with the body and extending into nature.

Photo Credits